WINNING TRACK AND FIELD DRILLS FOR WOMEN

TERRY CRAWFORD & BOB BERTUCCI

LEISURE PRESS

A publication of
Leisure Press
P.O. Box 3; West Point, N.Y. 10996

ISBN Number: 0-918438-95-0

Front cover photo: Steven E. Sutton/DUOMO
Front cover design: David Heberstreit

PHOTO CREDITS:
Don Gosney — 63, 69, 105
Dan Helms/DUOMO — 68
Paul J. Sutton/DUOMO — 8, 104
Steven E. Sutton/DUOMO — 9, 41
Athletic Journal — 29

■ CONTENTS

■ PREFACE

"For every action there is an equal and opposite reaction." Newton's third law, known as the law of reaction, is the cornerstone of proper mechanics and techniques in the sport of track and field.

Athletes constantly strive to maximize their performance. Drills provide the coach with a planned progression of skill attainment to maximize that performance. Moreover, innovative drills provide variety to the training routine and can be employed at all levels of performance.

Drills can be categorized as either developmental or corrective. Several basic principles should be followed in the design, selection, and implementation of any drill:

KEEP IT SIMPLE. Developmental drills should emphasize the fundamental aspects of a movement or the desired mechanical outcomes. They should also be designed to progress from simple to complex. Only a few drills should be selected to develop a single movement pattern. The athlete should be encouraged to execute the drill with precise movements. Developmental drills are best when integrated into the training routine regularly rather than when done sporadically. Mixing developmental drills into the warm-up routine is also an effective technique.

IF IT'S NOT BROKEN, DON'T FIX IT. Corrective drills must particularly adhere to this principle. The athletic skill must be qualitatively evaluated, the mechanical flaws identified, and the problem accurately pinpointed. It is important to be able to differentiate between style and technique. Proper technique can be defined as mechanically the most efficient movement sequence to accomplish a physical task. Style includes any other movements or characteristics of the motor pattern that do not adversely affect the efficiency of task execution. Therefore, it is sound advice not to change style unless under unusual circumstances, motor performance is undermined.

In addition to serving as a coaching and teaching aid, this book will hopefully inspire the reader to develop other drills to accomodate the particular needs of their athletes. One's imagination and ingenuity in applying simple motor tasks to the whole system of movement are the only limiting factors.

The contributors to this book are successful coaches with expertise in the respective events and in coaching the top ranked track athletes in the nation. The authors are grateful for their contribution to this collection of drills.

Terry Crawford
Head Track Coach
University of Texas

■CONTRIBUTORS

Terry Crawford
Head Track Coach
University of Texas

Sue Humphrey
Assistant Track Coach
University of Texas

Andrew Roberts
Assistant Track Coach
Syracuse University

Jan Seger
Research Consultant with Swedish
National Track Team

Loren Seagrave
Head Track Coach
Louisiana State University

Denise Wood
Assistant Track Coach
University of Tennessee

■ PART A

Track Drills

■ SECTION I

Basic Mechanics

TERRY CRAWFORD

Criss-Crossing Drill

PURPOSE
This drill develops balanced (arm and leg) action to aid efficient running mechanics. It also serves to align the body parts (on a straight line) and to emphasize and develop awareness of an aligned body while running.

DESCRIPTION
Over a distance of 50M to 150M, this drill is an over-emphasis of the bilateral action of the arms and legs. It should be started at a walk, and as it is repeated, speed can be increased to a fast skipping pace. Movement of the arms and legs should move through a full range, emphasizing a balanced and equal action. This drill should be repeated in sets of 4 at the prescribed distance and pace. Increase the distance as the pace increases.

SPECIAL INSTRUCTIONS
An excellent time to use this drill is during the warm-up and warm-down routine.

Terry Crawford

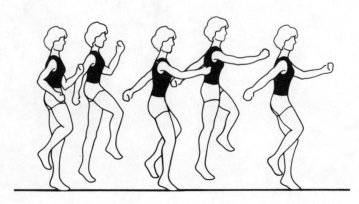

Hips Tall Position Drill

PURPOSE
This drill develops correct running and hurdle running positions.
DESCRIPTION
When done correctly, the athlete feels that the hips are as high off the ground as possible. The body support is high on the ball of the foot. The athlete also feels a sensation of being forward from just under the rib cage. Abdominals contract, and the back is relaxed and flat. An erect posture is maintained.

Loren Seagrave

"Running Tall" Drill

PURPOSE
This drill improves body alignment, enhances proper utilization of the respiratory system, and improves straight line drive in the arms and legs—thus allowing a full stride.

DESCRIPTION
Do this drill for a distance of 80 meters at three build-up speeds: slow, moderate, ¾ effort. Do three sets and have the runner stress a high chest and high hip carriage.

SPECIAL INSTRUCTIONS
Assumes the "hips tall" position:

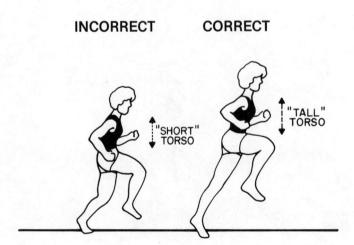

INCORRECT   CORRECT

"SHORT" TORSO

"TALL" TORSO

Hurdle Stepping Drill

PURPOSE
This drill is designed to require the athlete to recover the swing leg efficiently as a short lever.

DESCRIPTION
When the foot is pulled from the hurdle space, the heel must be drawn tight to the gluteus maximus. Failure to do this results in striking the hurdle. As the speed of the drill increases, the movement sequence becomes more automated until it reaches the point of being totally incorporated into the motor pattern. You may only use hurdles for this drill if you have the appropriate style Gill hurdles that have the bars situated so that a space for the foot exists at the 36" setting. You may also use velco hurdles. However, two straps per hurdle are needed to give the correct spacing. If neither of these options is available, fasten elastic cord to wooden 2 × 2's driven into the ground. The height should be no greater than 8 inches, and the distance between the 2 × 2's should be no greater than 18 inches. The athlete, in a running tall position, then executes a quick frequency high liner sprint action. This is performed so that the foot is placed between the bars of the hurdle. The athlete should stay high on the ball of the foot. The heel must be pulled out of the space by actively flexing the leg at the knee joint. A full range sprint arm action is mandatory.

SPECIAL INSTRUCTIONS
When learning this drill, the athletes can practice along the hurdles or cord. For less accomplished or coordinated athletes, cords are probably superior to hurdles. However, if the action is poorly executed the hurdle can remind the athlete of correct form and concentration.

Loren Seagrave

Line Drill for Form

PURPOSE
This drill teaches proper mechanics of the foot strike and proper alignment of the foot and knee through the driving phase of the stride.

DESCRIPTION
Using the lane lines on the track, the athlete straddles the lines for a distance of 50 meters. The straight line of movement is stressed by keeping the feet parallel to the line. The action of the knees should be high in front of the torso.

50 METERS

Back-Kick Drill

PURPOSE
This drill improves quickness of the leg action and emphasizes proper position of the back leg in the recovery phase of sprinting.

DESCRIPTION
For a distance of 30 meters, the runner emphasizes the back leg action of the stride. The heel of the foot should be brought up directly under the hips, actually touching the buttocks, and quickly jerked back to the track. The thigh remains perpendicular to the track; thus, all the action and movement of the leg is from the knee down. Alternate legs.

SPECIAL INSTRUCTIONS
This is an excellent drill for middle distance and distance runners, as well as sprinters, to improve "kicking" ability. The quickness of the back swing should be emphasized. A very small amount of ground should be covered with each step as the foot strikes the ground directly under the hip.

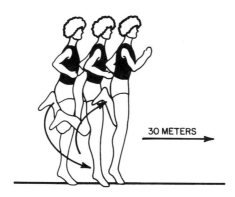

30 METERS

Hot-Track Drill

PURPOSE
This drill improves powerful push-off of the foot and improves and quickens the recovery phase of a stride.

DESCRIPTION
This drill is excellent for all runners, especially sprinters. With a loose, relaxed ankle, the athlete should run 50 meters at 60-75% effort. The athlete should use a stroking action with her foot, and her heels should never touch the track. Build up to three sets of four runs in a work-out session.

SPECIAL INSTRUCTIONS
The heel or lower leg should remain as closely in line with the center of gravity as possible; the foot and lower leg should not go back beyond the line of the hips.

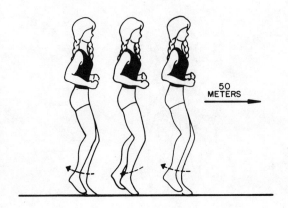

50
METERS

Harness Resistance Sprinting

PURPOSE

The purpose of this drill is to increase acceleration ability.

DESCRIPTION

A harness attached to an elastic cord or an automobile innertube attached to a rope is fastened around the athlete's waist or shoulders. The athlete then sprints at maximum effort against the cord, which is held by the coach or partner. The coach allows the athlete to make gradual forward progression to more closely simulate sprinting. The duration of the drill may be varied from ten seconds to one minute.

Loren Seagrave

Wall Sprint

PURPOSE
This drill integrates a new, faster neural firing pattern.

DESCRIPTION
The athlete assumes a hips tall position in a front support lean against a wall. The legs are driven in mechanically correct sprinting action. Responsiveness and tempo should be emphasized, and the mechanics of the leg should be carefully scrutinized.

SPECIAL INSTRUCTIONS
This exercise has many potential applications. It may be used by itself as a technical drill. It can also be incorporated with a sprint exercise circuit to emphasize mechanics and ground reaction. In addition, it may be used as a means of interval training in a confined area. Attaching elastic cords to the ankles provides an excellent strength development exercise for the hip and knee flexors. Care should be taken to allow the athlete to do build-ups or quick tempo running following this drill, particularly when cords are used.

Loren Seagrave

Frequency skipping

PURPOSE
This drill is designed to improve the athlete's frequency in running.

DESCRIPTION
The athlete jogs about 20 yards, then does very fast skipping movements for 20 yards. Arm work is done as in running. The athlete does this sequence for 100 yards, then rests, then repeats the drill three to four times. Tell the athlete that she is supposed to put her feet down as many times as possible in these 20 yards. (This means she is moving forward very slowly.)

To set a high pace for the leg movement, you can use a metronome over the loudspeaker.

Jan Seger

Stomp/Walk/Skip

PURPOSE

This drill emphasizes proper timing of hip and knee extension and flexion. It may also be used as a precursor to other plyometric exercises. This drill allows the athlete to experience the most efficient sprint mechanics in slow motion. It can also be expanded upon in other programs.

DESCRIPTION

The athlete maintains proper sprint posture through the entire drill. The proper sprint arm swing is in rhythm with the leg action. The Walk Rhythm emphasis is on the leg recovery phase, heel to butt and knee swing through. Little leg extension is apparent. A pause at the thigh parallel to the ground position is desired before hip extension. The Skip Rhythm emphasis is on the leg recovery and the hip extension phase so that a skipping rhythm is attained.

SPECIAL INSTRUCTIONS

The knee never exceeds 90° extension when the thigh is in full flexion. The skip uses forceful hip extension in conjunction with an active knee flexion.

The ground contact is under the body so that the shin angle is more acute than 90°. The foot is continually in a dorsi-flexed position. This drill should be implemented during a structured warm-up but can also be used in an interval spring session to emphasize proper sprint mechanics.

Loren Seagrave

Long Backward Strides

PURPOSE
This drill emphasizes the importance of knee flexion in the recovery of the swing leg. It also stimulates the sprint muscles in an antagonistic fashion which results in better total development of the sprinter.

The following hypothetical construction provides some of the philosophy behind this drill. If an athlete is able to excecute a reverse movement efficiently in a neuro-mechanically correct succession, the correct order would be facilitated. The strengthening of the antagonistic muscle group is equally important in determining the speed of execution of the movement.

DESCRIPTION
Several short backward running steps should be used to give momentum. The exact reverse order of running motion should be followed. Forceful hip flexion to propel the body backward is followed by simultaneous knee flexion and hip extension. Knee extension accompanies hip flexion before ground contact.

SPECIAL INSTRUCTIONS
Best implemented in a sprint exercise circuit.

Terry Crawford
Loren Seagrave

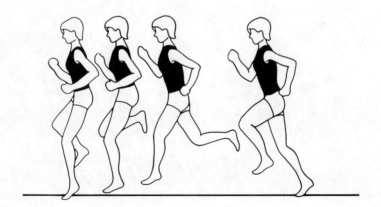

Stationary Arm Drill

PURPOSE

The purposes of this drill are to practice correct arm position when running, to emphasize a powerful backswing of the arm, and to show the athlete how powerful the arms can be in a full sprint movement. The arms alone will actually move the body from its starting spot.

DESCRIPTION

The athlete should be in a sitting position with her legs straight in front of her and her arms should be put in a running position by the side. The arms should be in a 90° angle at the elbow. With loosely clenched fists, the arm action starts at a slow tempo and gradually increases until the arms are driving at a full sprint tempo.

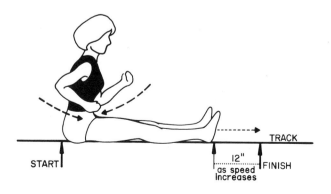

START TRACK 12" as speed increases FINISH

Warm-Down Skipping

PURPOSE

An excellent exercise after a speed work-out, this drill loosens the muscles and improves body coordination and rhythm.

DESCRIPTION

The athlete begins with a normal skipping action at a slow pace then increases the action to an over exaggerated motion of the arms and legs to have a longer non-support phase in the air. She does a 100M of skipping on straight-aways and jogging on the curves for 4 laps. The drill should be done at a relaxed and controlled pace.

Free Leg Swings (Front, Side and Figure Eight)

PURPOSE
This set of drills promotes dynamic flexibility of the hip joint.

DESCRIPTION
The athlete takes a hips tall position next to a wall or fence. The legs then swing freely from the hips. Front: during the extension, the leg flexes at the end of the range. This creates a short lever, so that when the thigh is flexed the leg extends at the low point. This action is similar to kicking a soccer ball. Side: the movement should be kept in the frontal plane, parallel to the shoulders, as much as possible. As the leg is abducted the hips swivel to allow a greater range of motion. Figure Eight: the leg circumscribes a figure eight loop in a plane, perpendicular to the shoulders. As the thigh is flexed, it swings inside out and loops around in front toward the body's midline. As the thigh is extended, it travels from inside-out, reversing the loop in the back.

Loren Seagrave

Fast Leg Drill (Alternate Rhythm)

PURPOSE
This drill is designed to develop quickness by isolating the leg recovery from the propulsion action. It also focuses on proper mechanics.

DESCRIPTION
While jogging in the hips tall position, the runner moves the leg through a stride cycle as quickly as possible. The sequence of steps can be described as shuffle-shuffle-quick step-shuffleshuffle-quick step.

The athlete executes the movement in a circular pattern.

Using the entire leg, the knee swings forward and upward through a full range of motion. The foot is dorsi-flexed, the thigh is extended forcefully, the leg is not actively extended, and the body is in the hips tall position. Arm action must mimic the leg's quick-full range of motion.

Loren Seagrave

Fast Leg Drill (Hurdle Rhythm)

PURPOSE
This drill stresses the active hip flexion-extension sequence in hurdling. It also allows the athlete to practice the light, shorter step on the trail leg prior to hurdle take-off.

DESCRIPTION
This variation of the fast leg drill differs from the previous drill only in rhythm, e.g. the stepping sequence remains the same.

This drill is best used with the hurdler's lead leg. The third step emphasis must be placed on a very short step, and the hurdler should be very high on the ball of the foot in an accentuated hips tall position.

SPECIAL INSTRUCTIONS
Place hurdle bars or baby hurdles at 5-6 meter intervals and then work the fast leg drill. Increase height progressively. Add trail leg action as height and skill dictate.

Loren Seagrave

Frequency running over marks

PURPOSE
This drill allows the athlete to practice keeping a stride length.

DESCRIPTION
Put marks out on the track. The distance between marks should be 50, 60, 70, 80, 90, 100, 110, 120, 130, 140, 150, 160, 170, 180, 190, 200, ... cm. The runner starts about 20 yards before the first mark and tries to find and maintain a good frequency. During the drill, she changes only the stride length. After the last mark she runs about 20-30 yards keeping the same frequency and stride length. The running position is important.

Jan Seger

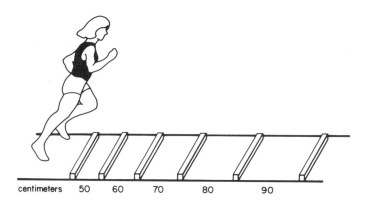

centimeters   50   60   70   80   90

Running with elastic ribbon

PURPOSE
This drill increases speed and improves coordination in high velocity running.

DESCRIPTION
An elastic cord (about 30-40 yards long) is tied at about the 50 yard line. The runner places the cord around the back of her hips and backs up until the cord is stretched. She runs from a high start for about 50 yards at maximum speed. She will get an increase in speed from the elasticity of the cord. It's important that the runner keeps a good running position during the drill.

Jan Seger

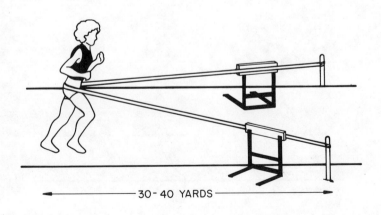

30-40 YARDS

MODEL FOR THE CROUCH START SET POSITION

SIDE VIEW

Major Cues:
Shoulders above the hands
Hips slightly above the shoulders
Front leg no less than 90°
Rear leg about 120°
Shins approximately parallel, at a low angle to track
Front two spikes of shoes on track

FRONT VIEW

Major Cues:
Thumbs under shoulders
Support on fingers, make a high bridge
Feet on pedals, under hips
Slightly more weight supported by the power side arm (front leg)

MOVEMENT SEQUENCE

Major Cues:
1. Quick side elbow initiates movement, drive back.
2. Power side forearm drives up, not out.
3. Quick side and power side leg simultaneously extend from the hip make the block slide back along the ground.
4. Quick side leg recovery.
   a. Knee drives low and forward
   b. Shin does not fold-up
   c. Long lever power action
   d. Heel does not come to gluteus
5. Power side leg continues to extend explosively 6. Airborne phase— project hips out in a jackknife action from hip and back extensors.
   a. Contact point behind center of gravity
   b. Foot moves backward at ground contact
   c. Knee angle is greater than 90%; on impact the shin angle must be acute with respect to the ground
   d. Quickside leg extends forcefully from the hip

6. Airborne phase—project hips out in a jackknife action from hip and back extensors.
   a. Contact point behind center of gravity
   b. Foot moves backward at ground contact
   c. Knee angle is greater than 90%; on impact the shin angle must be acute with respect to the ground.
   d. Quickside leg extends forcefully from the hip.

■ SECTION II

Sprint Starts

LOREN SEAGRAVE

Partner Push Drill

PURPOSE
This drill allows the athlete to experience the start of a sprint with the arm drive slightly preceeding the bilateral leg drive and the quick side leg recovery. Also, the drill allows the coach to evaluate the efficiency of the start. The more efficient the starting position, the more forceful will be the push.

DESCRIPTION
The athlete is positioned in the proper set position. The partner or coach stands in front of the crouched sprinter. He places his hands on the starter's shoulders and assumes a braced position. On command, the athlete dives explosively into a fully extended position. The coach provides resistance and support.

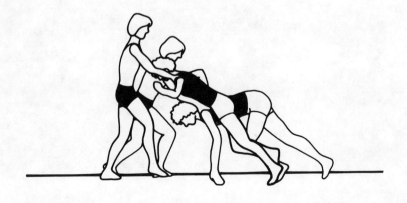

Elbow Drive Drill (Kneeling Position Variation)

PURPOSE

The practice of motor set. Attention is focused on the movement to be made in response to the stimulus, rather than the sensory set. This is paramount in yielding the shortest reaction time. In addition, the movement program must be initiated by the quick side arm. No forward propulsion of the body's center of mass can result as long as the arms are in contact with the ground. The focus on the elbow drive movement allows this to happen.

DESCRIPTION

In the first phase of this drill the athlete is in the "On your mark position" with the weight of the body supported mostly by the legs. The pendulum ball or knotted sweatsuit is suspended behind the quick-side shoulder. The quick-side is the side that has the foot furthest from the line. The command "set" is given so that the athlete can properly prepare a pre-motor mental set of conditions. The pre-motor mental set focuses the athletes attention on the movement to be made at the sound of the gun. The focal movement is forceful extension at the shoulder so that the elbow is driven toward and strikes the pendulum ball. The action is analogous to the reaction of touching an unexpectedly very hot item such as an iron or the handle of a frying pan. Even though the flexor reflex at the elbow rather than the arm extensors is called upon to withdraw the hand, the disynaptic quickness of the response elicited gives the athlete a good mental image of the action. On the go command, the movement is performed at maximum effort.

SPECIAL INSTRUCTIONS

To better facilitate the recovery drive of the quick side elbow, support of the body's weight on the arms should be disproportionately distributed in favor of the power side arm. This has two purposes. It not only reduces the weight on the quick-side arm allowing it to be withdrawn efficiently and more quickly, but also shifts the center of mass within the frontal plane more in line with the leg, which will be applying force over the greatest period of time. This will eliminate the stepping from side to side so often seen in powerful starters.

Elbow Drive Drill
(Set Position Variation)

PURPOSE
Same as the Elbow Drill kneeling position.

DESCRIPTION
The arm action in response to the go command remains the same. The pendulum ball should be held in a position so that when the athlete drives the hips forward and the body is in a power-line position, it may be struck by the elbow. In addition, a dual premotor set may be used. The focus on the elbow drive backwards may be accompanied by a bilateral extension from the hip. The drive from both legs against the blocks maximizes the force exerted, hence maximizes the acceleration of the body. The quick and responsive extension of the rear leg from the hip is an action which in most cases must be taught. The full range drive from the power-side leg is a more intuitive action. Extension force must come predominantly from the hip rather than the knee. The athlete can visualize applying the force so that if the blocks were not anchored to the floor, they would be driven back, sliding along the ground. This total response results in the full execution of the sprint start.

SPECIAL INSTRUCTIONS
To enhance the extension of the rear leg, the verbal "go" command is substituted with a tactile stimulus. The coach kneels on the quick side next to the athlete and touches the athlete behind the quick side knee. The coach should be conscious to avoid being struck by the athlete's quick side arm drive or spiked in the hand during the recovery phase of the quick side leg. The athlete immediately extends the leg from the hip in an effort to push against the finger's light pressure. It is important not to eliminate the arm drive which is the slight predecessor movement.

Jack Knife Start Drill

PURPOSE
To successfully accomplish the drill requires that the athlete project the hips forward while simultaneously extending explosively from the back. This results in the line position, through which force may be applied. Many times athletes do not extend and project fully due to their fear of falling. The correct resultant position is very much out of balance, with the center of mass far in front of the support base. This however, is necessary for optimal acceleration.

DESCRIPTION
The athlete enters the blocks and rises into the proper set position.

A soft object is suspended one foot above and two feet in front of the athlete's head. The most desirable object is a pair of sweat pants with a knot tied at the waist.

The athlete has been instructed to extend forcefully from the hip and back, so that the object is struck with the upper back.

SPECIAL INSTRUCTIONS
This should be used only as a corrective drill and is best implemented early in the training session before competitions.

Don't Kick The Ball Start Drill

PURPOSE

One of the most important factors in learning a new motor pattern or in changing an established motor pattern is for the athlete to receive immediate and accurate knowledge of results (KR). KR need not always be positive as with the Jack Knife Start Drill.

The action of folding the shin-up while recovering the quick side leg has several adverse effects.

1) The amount of time taken before ground contact is greater when the foot is recovered high by folding the shin up against the thigh. This is not desirable.

2) Folding the shin also allows the hips to settle into a position lower than the body can handle. This is the prime cause for the weak, sinking feeling experienced on step two, three or four.

3) The tendency for the athlete to reach out forward with the foot is increased by the shin folding and hence the lever shortening. This is very inefficient in trying to maintain as good body position for accelerating since the contact point usually is in front of the center of gravity.

DESCRIPTION

The same soft object used in the Jack Knife Start Drill is suspended one foot above the quick side (rear) leg, while the athlete is in the blocks. The athlete rises into the set position. On command or at will the athlete explodes from the blocks. If the object is kicked by the quick side heel the force application and recovery of the quick side leg was incorrect.

SPECIAL INSTRUCTIONS

This drill should be used only as a corrective drill and is best implemented early in the training season before competition.

Pole Vault Pit Starts

PURPOSE
The optimal application of force comes from a simultaneous extension of both legs from the hips. Often the athlete receives no push from the rear leg. This drill also emphasizes that the arms initiate the action. Both legs actually apply force against the blocks while the arms are off the ground. It is a decided disadvantage for the rear leg to sneak out while the hands are in contact with the ground.

DESCRIPTION
The athlete sets the blocks so that a starting line rests three feet from the angled front section of the pole vault pit. On command the athlete dives with the arms out and extends powerfully from both hips, projecting the hips forward and upward slightly. The athlete lands in the pole vault pit in the prone position. A long sleeve shirt should be worn in this drill to protect the athlete's elbows.

SPECIAL INSTRUCTIONS
Best results are obtained if Pole Vault Pit Starts are mixed with regular maximum effort starts.

3 FEET

Falling Starts

PURPOSE

This drill puts the athlete's body in the accelerating position. It promotes placement of each successive step in the proper position behind the center of mass for the most efficient acceleration.

DESCRIPTION

The athlete assumes a standing start position with the back leg against the pedal of the back block (Note: the blocks are set for that athlete). The back leg should be in almost full hip extension. The front leg is placed just beyond the starting line so that when a power line position (a line from the ankle of the back leg through the knee, hip and shoulder) is taken, the body is balanced. The arms are opposite the legs and ready to drive on command. On the command, the front leg is picked up and moved backward as close to the front block as possible. This should be done without breaking the power line position. At contact, the athlete drives explosively and accelerates down the track.

SPECIAL INSTRUCTIONS

The drill may be slightly modified so that the first step from the blocks may be practiced. In this case the powerside leg is positioned against the block and the power line position assumed. Support is then on the quick side leg. On command the quick side leg is picked up and placed back behind the starting line. Acceleration automatically ensues.

Stand Starts

PURPOSE
This is an exercise in acceleration. The objective is to increase the strength and power of the athlete and at the same time develop new, more explosive movement patterns.

DESCRIPTION
The athlete stands with the powerside leg forward. The spacing between the feet is one foot length measured from the heel of the power side to the toe of the quick side. In the set position the athlete bends forward from the trunk. The front (powerside) leg is flexed at the knee as much as possible. The athlete is on the balls of the feet. The arms are in a position opposite the legs. On the command the athlete drives with the arms and legs to attain maximum acceleration.

Deep Start Drill

PURPOSE
This exercise is designed to be a power development drill. Both the front and rear legs must drive through a greater range of motion than required in the block start. In addition, a weight vest or belt may be used to progressively increase resistance.

DESCRIPTION
The athlete takes a position similar to the "On your mark position." Starting blocks and spikes may be used. The powerside leg is in a position such that the knee almost touches the elbow of the support arm. On the command or at will, the athlete explodes from both legs and bounds three to four steps.

Push-up Starts

PURPOSE
The purpose of this drill is to improve the strength and coordination of both arm and leg action during the track start. Improved strength and coordination results in increased efficiency of movement.

DESCRIPTION
The athlete assumes a normal push-up position. From this position, the knees are lowered to the track. The power side leg (front leg) is then moved forward so that the foot approximates the opposite knee. The rear foot then is moved to a position about twelve inches behind the front foot. The athlete rises into the set position. On the command, go, the athlete executes the start.

Harness Starts

PURPOSE

This drill provides a very specific resistance exercise. It also allows the athlete to experience longer force application time against the blocks. This in turn can be used to focus on rear leg drive and extension from the hip rather than the knee.

DESCRIPTION

An elastic cord is attached to a harness. The harness is fastened around the athlete's waist. The proper set position is assumed. On the command the athlete drives against the blocks and accelerates down the track against the resistance of the cord. A long elastic cord should be used so that long smooth resistant pull is obtained. If only a short cord is available, the coach or partner must move forward with the athlete to allow smooth acceleration.

SPECIAL INSTRUCTIONS

If the athlete has problems projecting their hips forward by forceful extension of their thigh, the cord should be attached to the waist.

■ SECTION III

Hurdles

LOREN SEAGRAVE

CUES TO PROPER TRAIL LEG ACTION WHILE HURDLING

- At take-off, the heel is pulled tight to the buttocks.
- The foot is in dorsi-flexion, ankle everted.
  (Cue: bend ankle to ear)
- The knee swings through forward and upward.
- The knee stays as close to the body as possible.
  (Cue: Knee under arm pit)
- The knee continues to be driven forward until the thigh is to the front, pointing down the track in sprint form. The leg remains tightly folded against the thigh. The lower leg never extends past a position which is parallel to the ground.
- Powerful hip extension, causes the leg to explode into the ground. The Hips Tall Position is maintained after the hurdle.

CUES TO PROPER LEAD LEG ACTION

- At take off, the heel is pulled tight to the gluteus maximus.
- The knee rapidly swings through forward.
  (Cue: Hurdle with the knee)
- The leg remains tightly folded against thigh until the thigh is parallel to ground. The leg is whipped into extension (Karate Kick Action) by the rapid deceleration of the thigh.
- During the attack action the foot remains dorsi-flexed.
  (Cue: toe-up) This tip keeps the leg tight against the thigh.
- The thigh is extended powerfully from the hip, while the leg flexes quickly at the knee in reflex response to the violent action of #3.
- The thigh continues to be extended forcefully. This causes the foot to pull backward into the ground and directly under the body so that a Hips Tall and Forward Position is maintained off the hurdle.

Trail Knee Pick-ups

PURPOSE

This dynamic flexibility exercise is specifically related to the task of hurdling.

DESCRIPTION

The hurdler takes the hurdle seat stretch position. The body lean is accentuated in conjunction with the lead arm driving forward. Simultaneously the trail leg knee is lifted as high as possible off the ground. The trail leg toe, out of necessity remains on the ground.

SPECIAL INSTRUCTIONS

This drill is best used in a dynamic flexibility circuit.

Twisters

PURPOSE

This provides dynamic flexibility in the trunk and hips that is essential in hurdling.

DESCRIPTION

The athlete takes a wide stradle position with the arms outstretched from the shoulders. In a rhythmic cadence, the athlete twists so that the left arm touches behind the right knee. The right arm to the left knee follows.

Front Eagle

PURPOSE
This exercise promotes dynamic flexibility in the hip joint. This can be used in a flexibility circuit or as a preparation for sprinting or hurdling.

DESCRIPTION
The athlete assumes a prone position on the track with the horizontal axis of the shoulders resting on a lane line. The arms are outstretched in the same axis along the lane line. While trying to maintain shoulder contact with the track, the leg is extended so that the right toe reaches over the back to touch the left hand. This is followed by the left toe and the right hand.

LANE LINE

Back Eagle

PURPOSE
Same as for Front Eagle
DESCRIPTION
The athlete assumes a supine position similar to the Front Eagle position. The right leg then swings dynamically over to touch the left hand. Following the return, the left leg swings over to the right hand.

LANE LINE

Trail Leg Windmill

PURPOSE
To further develop the proper motor pattern of the hurdle trail leg.

To enhance dynamic flexibility and joint suppleness throughout the full range of motion and at speeds exceeding the speed of movement during actual hurdle clearance.

DESCRIPTION
A front support position against the wall is assumed and an attempt to maintain the Hips Tall position is made. The proper trail leg action is executed in rapid succession. Common faults to watch:

1) The heel drifting away from a tight position against the thigh.
2) The knee not being pulled up and forward. Many times the upward emphasis is neglected. This sets the athlete up for a flicking leg action, which can lead to medial knee pain if not corrected.
3) The foot is not held in a dorsi-flexed position.
4) The foot is not everted causing little to no external rotation of the thigh. This will also cause the toe to hit the hurdle.

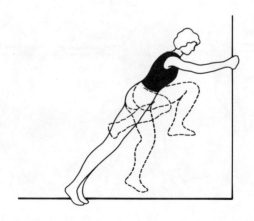

Hurdle Seat Change

PURPOSE
This exercise is a specific dynamic flexibility exercise which can be used in a warm-up during a flexibility circuit or as a special preparation prior to hurdling.

DESCRIPTION
The hurdle seat position is assumed by the athlete. The right leg is extended as if it were the lead leg. The athlete then rolls to the right through a front support position. Simultaneously, the left leg is extended to become the new lead leg. As the athlete continues to roll, the right heel is pulled quickly to the buttocks so that it becomes the new trail leg. Once the left leg lead hurdle seat is accomplished the athlete then lowers the chest onto the leg. The athlete then reverses the action rolling back to the left.

Stationary Trail Leg Half Hurdling (Three step rhythm)

PURPOSE
This is a very specific dynamic flexibility exercise. It also insures that the trail leg remains tucked tightly against the thigh and does not open up. It must be returned directly under the body.

DESCRIPTION
The athlete stands facing the hurdle so that a perpendicular line from the outside edge of the hurdle would bisect the mid-line of the body. The trail leg should be covered by the hurdle. The lead leg steps and is placed slightly past the hurdle. The trail leg is brought through quickly, staying tight to the body. Three backward shuffle steps, which have the characteristics of the three stride rhythm, returns the athlete to the start position.

ADVANCED DRILL
Stationary Trail Leg Half Hurdling (Continuous rhythm)
This drill is identical to the three stride rhythm drill, but does not have the three recovery strides. The trail leg action is executed only to be repeated in the next cycle.

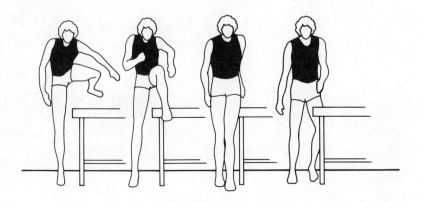

Trail Leg Circle

PURPOSE
This is an excellent drill for the young hurdler. It allows the hurdler to focus on the proper recovery action of the trail leg and promotes dynamic flexibility.

DESCRIPTION
The athlete stands in the Hips Tall Position so that the hurdle rests to the trail leg side. The lead leg is positioned slightly beyond the hurdle. The trail leg knee is then pulled up and forward executing the trail leg action. The action must be so cyclical and the leg so tightly flexed against the thigh, that upon thigh extension of the trail leg, the foot returns to the original starting position.

Lead and Trail Leg Half-Hurdling

PURPOSE
To increase velocity and acceleration off the barrier as well as increase stride frequency.

DESCRIPTION
The hurdles are positioned at the desired spacing so they sit completely within a lane. The athlete is positioned to straddle one of the adjacent lane lines. Running the normal three stride rhythm, the hurdler negotiates the barrier with only the lead leg, bringing the trail leg through quickly along the side of the barrier. The trail leg version is preceeded by a quick lead leg action that lands past the hurdle.

SPECIAL INSTRUCTIONS
This drill provides excellent preparation for hurdle training sessions. Often, reduced spacing should be employed. Some hurdlers will find a five stride rhythm useful. Care should be taken when using five strides not to be too close to the hurdle at take off.

Trail Leg Hurdle Walk/Skip-Overs

PURPOSE
To emphasize the proper mechanics under controlled conditions. To allow the athlete to experience the quick, cyclical action of the trail leg. To integrate the arms with the Trail Leg, in order to execute the hurdle action sooner and achieve the sprint position.

DESCRIPTION
5-12 hurdles are placed at a distance of about 1.70m, depending on the athlete's height and level of development. This is also true for the height of the hurdle.

The athlete begins (and maintains) the exercise in a Hips Tall position throughout the set of hurdles. The athlete stands in this position when walking the hurdles so that only the trail leg must negotiate the barrier.

The proper trail leg and arm action is executed while negotiating the row of hurdles. The range of movement is also emphasized.

Advanced skipping technique.

Once the athlete has mastered the walk-over aspect, a more dynamic movement may be practiced by using a quicker skipping rhythm.

Time of year: All Phases.

Implementation: This can be used as preparation for hurdling workouts but may also act as a technique training session.

Lead Leg Tapping

PURPOSE
This drill is a specific dynamic flexibility exercise best suited for a preparatory hurdle circuit.

DESCRIPTION
The hurdle is placed at a height between 12 and 33 inches depending on the skill level and the height of the athlete. The athlete is positioned 6 inches from the barrier with the shoulder axis perpendicular to the hurdle. Beginning the action from the Hips Tall position, the lead leg is positioned next to the hurdle rail, and in front of the body. The lead leg is then flexed quickly at the hip and knee so that the leg may be moved across the barrier and placed on the other side. This movement is executed back and forth to a rhythmic hopping action while maintaining the Hips Tall position. The arms should follow the action to maintain balance.

SPECIAL INSTRUCTIONS
It is important to keep the knee joint flexed so that the heel can be brought back to the buttocks. The leg must not be moved over the hurdle in an extended position.

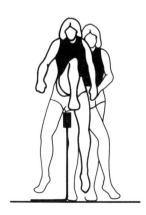

Lead Leg Wall Drill

PURPOSE
The most significant benefit of this drill is achieving the shortened, quick stride of the trail leg in preparation for attacking the hurdle (penultimate stride). This is paramount in achieving the correct low flight parabola and in deminishing the vertical impulse of the hurdle stride. This stride must be very "light" with the foot placed abnormally close under the center of mass. However, the heel never touches this mass. The post support phase of the contact time is maximized, thus lending critical forward rotation to the body. This rotation hastens the return of the lead leg to the track and the application of propulsive force.

DESCRIPTION
There are two stages to this drill. The first begins with the athlete's trail leg forward. The weight of the body is disproportionately supported by the lead leg behind the athlete. The sequence of action is as follows: The athlete drives off the lead leg into a hips tall position. The athlete's focus is to drive through the trail leg, rather than off the trail leg. This requires a short support phase on the trail leg. The lead knee is driven at an imaginary hurdle rail two meters away on the wall. The proper arm action is excuted.

The second stage finds the athlete six to eight meters from the wall with the feet in the same starting position. A stride is taken onto the lead leg. An effort is made to drive to the hurdle from the lead leg. The trail leg takes a very abbreviated stride, and support is very high on the ball of the foot. The hips are in a tall position. The knee of the lead leg is simultaneously driven toward the wall with the lower leg extending only in response to the abrupt decleration of the thigh.

SPECIAL INSTRUCTIONS
The fast leg drill is an excellent lead-up drill toward development of a quick light approach step.

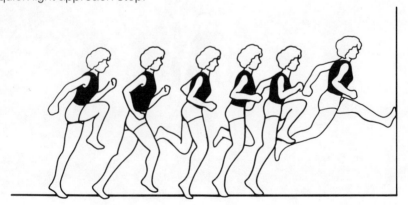

Take-off Sensation Drill

PURPOSE
Experiencing the proper take-off position gives the athlete a sense of a low take off angle necessary to minimize execution time of the hurdle stride.

DESCRIPTION
The athlete stands facing the coach with both hands on the coach's shoulders. The coach holds the athlete's lead leg just above the knee. The leg is bent at the knee and the foot is dorsi-flexed. The coach backs slightly away from the athlete and lifts up the lead knee to put the athlete in a forward leaning Hips Tall position.

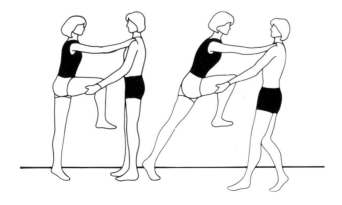

Stair Step Hurdling

PURPOSE
This is an excellent adjunct to the fast leg hurdle rhythm drill. It may also be used to vary indoor training or to break up a power development training session on the stairs.

DESCRIPTION
Using an ordinary flight of stairs, the hurdler climbs them using a one-one-one-two pattern, which reflects the demands in hurdling. The negotiation of two steps is obviously done with the preferred lead leg. The step before the hurdle stride must be quickened and the body put in a hips tall position. The arms move through a full range of motion to mirror the demands on the legs.

SPECIAL INSTRUCTIONS
Often times regular steps may be too high for young hurdlers or shorter hurdlers. In this case stadium steps which provide half step increments are desirable.

Rhythm Drills

Most hurdlers take approximately the same number of strides over the course of the 100m or 110m hurdle race. The divisions are seven or eight strides to the first hurdle, three strides between hurdles (yielding 27), ten hurdle strides and four to six strides from the last hurdle to the finish for a total of 48-51 strides.

The time required to cover the flat distance (without hurdles) is a product of stride length and stride frequency. Hurdles impose a definite and hazzardous restriction on stride length, therefore reduction of the total time is dependent on increasing the stride frequency. The total time can be divided into four catagories,

1) The time required to reach the first hurdle.
2) The time required to negotiate the ten hurdle strides.
3) The time required to cover the distance between hurdles.
4) The time needed from the last hurdle to the finish.

The first is a function of power production capability and efficient acceleration mechanics.

The second is a function of mechanically efficient execution of the hurdle stride, which has been the subject of the previous drills.

The latter can be improved with the following drills.

Hurdlers Knee Clap Drill

PURPOSE
To simulate the straight forward position of the body through the barrier. Emphasis should be placed on the high knee action necessary for hurdle clearance. This drill allows the student to practice the sprint-hurdle action and at the same time teaches proper body balance and position.

DESCRIPTION
The athlete stands on the balls of the feet with hands raised chest high, palms down, and elbows bent. The athlete must raise knee to palm with very quick leg action in the hurdle rhythm. The athlete should begin the drill over a distance of 40m and as balance and timing improves extend the distance to 100m. The drill should be repeated 3-4 times in a training routine.

SPECIAL INSTRUCTIONS
The coach should emphasize that the athlete use a short step that does not cover much distance. Avoid the tendency to lean backward when bringing the knees up to the hands by maintaining correct sprint form with the proper amount of forward lean and complete extension of the driving leg.

Andy Roberts

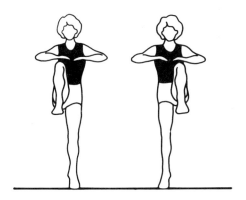

Hand Clap Hurdle Rhythm

PURPOSE

This drill allows the athlete to progressively internalize the rhythm and cadence required to run the hurdles successfully. It also adds an auditory dimension to the process of imagery and visualization.

DESCRIPTION

The athlete sits on the ground with both legs fully extended to the front. The athlete then claps the three stride hurdle rhythm at various tempos. Once this is mastered the athlete claps the entire 60 yard hurdle race. Seven or eight strides to the first hurdle followed by clearance and between strides of five hurdles and the run-in. The next step is to clap the 100m hurdle race. Visualization and imagery are added as the athlete becomes more proficient in executing the task.

Andy Roberts

Arm Swing Hurdle Rhythm

PURPOSE

This drill helps the athlete further internalize the rhythm pattern and cadence of the hurdle race. In addition, the drill more closely emulates the action of hurdling so that more accurate visualization can be attached to kinesthetic cues from the arm action. The "exaggerated", full range of motion of the arms, leads into the quick, short stroke action of the sprint between the hurdles. This response is particularly difficult to elicit while actually sprinting over the barriers.

DESCRIPTION

The athlete sits on the ground with both legs fully extended to the front. The hurdler then drives the arms in a sprint action at varying frequencies. The hurdle rhythm is then added accentuating the action of the lead arm, and incorporating a slight internal rotation of the shoulder. This is followed by a quick arm reverse, with the lead arm elbow being forcefully driven backward and the trail arm swinging tightly forward from the shoulder. The entire hurdle action is terminated with the next full range movement of the arms. This last cycle corresponds with the powerful extension from the hip of the already recovered trail leg.

Andy Roberts

Reduced Space Hurdling

PURPOSE
Often times in a training environment the level of activation, excitement, or arousal is much less than in the arena of competition. Reducing the space between the hurdle allows or even forces the athlete to run using a reduced stride length which, in turn, facilitates greater stride frequency. Velocity curves generated from high level women hurdlers show that most female athletes are able to accelerate to hurdle five in the 80m hurdles (12m to the first, 8.00m between.) However, curves from the 100m hurdles show that only elite athletes are able to produce this acceleration pattern. This principle also applies for male hurdlers.

An additional benefit of reduced space hurdling allows the athlete to experience the hips tall position, using a quick, shortened, light step onto the trail leg in preparation for the hurdle stride. The fear of being too far away from the hurdle is markedly diminished.

DESCRIPTION
The interval between the hurdles is reduced to 7.80m—8.50 for females and 8.50m—9.00 for males. The interval used is dependent on the ability of the athlete, track and weather conditions, the intensity of the workout and the level of activation or excitement of the athlete, which is enhanced by a competitive or semi-competitive situation.

SPECIAL INSTRUCTIONS
Unless a marked tail wind or a very competitive workout situation exists, most hurdling can be done with reduced spacing. As the year progresses, the reduction may be reduced to more closely approximate the normal distance.

Reduced Height Hurdling

PURPOSE
The use of a reduced height hurdle allows the athlete to markedly decrease hurdle clearance time. This requires that the hurdle stride action be executed earlier and more quickly in the hurdle stride. The lower the hurdle, the sooner the action must be completed so that the post-hurdle lead leg support time is reduced. An additional benefit is the noticeable increase in stride frequency between the hurdles.

DESCRIPTION
The height of the hurdle is reduced to 20-27 inches for females and from 33-40 inches for males depending on expertise, leg length and age of hurdler.

Image Hurdling

PURPOSE
To increase stride frequency between the hurdles as well as decrease the time required to execute the hurdle stride. This drill is especially effective with less experienced hurdlers.

DESCRIPTION
Sections of wood similar to the top hurdle bar are placed on the track at intervals of between 8.00m and 8.50m depending on the athlete's ability and weather conditions. The athlete, from the starting blocks, sprints at full effort, emphasizing a quick three stride rhythm. The hurdle stride is executed as if a hurdle was present. Emphasis is placed on shortening the flight time and flight distance by completing the hurdle stride early.

SPECIAL INSTRUCTIONS
This drill may be used in conjunction with block start work or as a work out in itself. With more experienced hurdlers, alternating Image Hurdling, Reduced Height Hurdling and Reduced Space Hurdling can subtly effect change.

Race the Sprinter

PURPOSE
The ability to continue to accelerate to the fourth and fifth hurdle is essential for high level results. This requires proper sprint posture and attitude coming off and, more importantly, going into the hurdle. The powerful hip extension required of the lead leg prior to and during ground contact after the hurdle, is of paramount importance. In addition, rapid and early execution of the hurdle stride results in the trail leg being in the proper position to extend powerfully immediately after lead leg contact.

Minimum differences should be the goal between 20m—40 yard flat times and the three hurdle conditions. Other useful comparison times include the third hurdle touch down time, the block start 30m flat times and the flying 30m flat time with an interval beginning at the trail leg contact before the second hurdle and ending at the 50 meter mark. Four hurdles are used for the latter test.

DESCRIPTION
Under competitive circumstances, a sprinter starts from blocks next to a hurdler. The hurdler has either no hurdle, one hurdle, two hurdles or three hurdles to negotiate. Commands and gun starts are given by a starter. The race distance covered is 40 yards. Times are recorded at the 20 meter mark and the 40 yard.

16 Meter Start Hurdling

PURPOSE

The maximum velocity at the first hurdle is greater using the extended start. This provides two benefits. The ground contact time before and after the hurdle must be reduced to handle the higher velocity. The second parameter affected is the hurdle clearance time. Because of the increased velocity, the hurdle stride must be executed sooner so that the proper sprint position is reached prior to lead leg ground contact. The use of drills such as this subtly teach the body to adapt to conditions of artificially enhanced performance. This allows a breakthrough and reduction of component times, resulting in an improved overall time.

DESCRIPTION

For female hurdlers, a 16m distance rather than 13 meters is used to the first hurdle. Adjustments may have to be made for a seven stride approach hurdler. For male hurdlers a 19 yard distance is the norm rather than the actual 15 yard start. Again, there may be slight variation for a seven stride approach.

Five Stride Rhythm Hurdling

PURPOSE

The increased spacing allows the athlete additional time to accelerate between the hurdles thus yielding a higher hurdle clearance velocity. This mandates reduced ground contact time before the hurdle and allows a significantly increased stride frequency between hurdles.

SPECIAL INSTRUCTIONS

A seven stride rhythm may occasionally be used at 14.50m-15.50m for females and 19—205 yards for males, however the tendency to increase the stride length beyond the mean length demanded for the event, 1.80m-1.90m for females and approximately 2 yards 4 inches for males usually outweighs any possible advantage.

Hurdle endurance work-out

PURPOSE
Practice endurance indoors (300m—400m hurdles)

DESCRIPTION
The hurdler runs 100m hurdles (a), then walks over hurdles (b)— technique drill. After 2-3 minutes rest the athlete runs the 100m hurdles back (c). Rest 5-6 minutes. Repeat 3-6 times. The speed is submaximal (90% of maximum). Male hurdlers run on 100cm and 91.4cm hurdles. Female hurdlers run on 84.0cm and 76.2cm hurdles.

Jan Seger

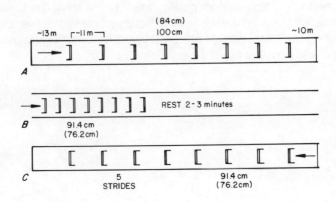

Rhythm Endurance Hurdling

PURPOSE
The importance of rhythm maintenance in the 100m and 110m hurdles is paramount. Mechanically efficient hurdle clearance allows reduced deceleration into the hurdle on the pre-hurdle trail leg step and on the lead leg landing off the hurdle. The sprint hurdler falls victim to the same peril as the 100 meter sprinter of gradually increasing stride length accompanied by decreasing stride frequency in the last 40-50 meters of the race. Obviously, this is undesirable for the hurdler. Progressively reducing the height and the spacing of the hurdles allows, and to some extent, forces the hurdler to maintain a high running rhythm.

This rhythm maintenance is accomplished by:
1) Maintaining the hips tall position and shortening the stride prior to the hurdle.
2) Executing the hurdle action early in the hurdle stride, allowing the lead foot to contact the ground under the hips, preventing deceleration, and reducing the post hurdle lead leg support time.
3) Preventing the trail leg shin from opening prematurely, thus avoiding a breaking effect.
4) Preventing a shin opening and reaching out in front of the body on the strides between the hurdles.

DESCRIPTION
The hurdle heights and spacing are reduced progressively at various key points in the race. This is dependant on level of ability, weather and track conditions, and fitness level of the athlete. Several useful patterns are listed below using the 100m-33″ hurdle.

HURDLE #1–33″, #2 & # 3—30″ @ 8.25m,
#4–# 6—30″ @ 8.00m,
#7–#10—27″ @ 7.80m,

HURDLE #1–33″, # 2 & # 3—33″ @ 8,25m,
4–# 6—30″ @ 8.25m,
7–# 9—30″ @ 8.00m,
8–#10—27″ @ 8.00m,
#11–#12—24″ @ 7.80m.

SPECIAL INSTRUCTIONS
Rhythm endurance hurdling is best incorporated into the training early in the competitive indoor season, (i.e., January or February) and again early in the competitive outdoor season.

Variable Stride Hurdling

PURPOSE
This variable stride requirement reduces the likelihood of developing a stereotyped rhythm. This permits greater potential for breakthrough and improvement in technique and overall performance.

DESCRIPTION
The distance between the hurdles is varied between a one stride (extended to 4.5m), three stride and five stride requirement.

SPECIAL INSTRUCTION
One stride and variable stride hurdling is best practiced with velcro or safety hurdles. Your athletes and your trainer will thank you.

One Stride Rhythm Hurdling

PURPOSE
The immediacy of the up-coming barrier requires the athlete to respond almost reflexively with the lead leg. This further engrains the motor pattern of the hurdle stride action and early execution of the action.

DESCRIPTION
The hurdles are placed at a distance of approximately 4 meters apart. The hurdler is allowed either a 3 stride or 5 stride approach depending on the competence of the hurdler. While maintaining a hips tall position throughout, the hurdler negotiates the barriers using proper lead leg and trail leg mechanics with only one step between. This drill is best carried out with reduced height hurdles.

■ SECTION IV

Distance Running

TERRY CRAWFORD

Tennessee Shockers— for middle distance and distance runners

PURPOSE
To simulate race conditions of changing pace. To develop surging tactics and condition the athlete to hold a steady state tempo after an anaerobic bout of exercise.

DESCRIPTION
9 Minutes of intermittent surges within a continuous run. Preferably this exercise should be done on a 440 yard track or grassy area. The runner responds to the coach's whistle command moving through 3 speed:

    steady state pace (10K pace)—1 whistle

    tempo run—(mile race pace)—2 whistles

    sprint pace—3 whistles

    The coach controls the pace based on the whistle command.

SPECIAL INSTRUCTIONS
Initially this drill should be done with one 9 minute drill. As conditioning improves, 2 sets of 9 minute runs can be conducted in one work-out session. Allow 7-8 minutes rest between the sets. As the speed increases, the amount of time the runner is held in that phase should diminish.

Indian File

PURPOSE
To promote group running. This drill also adds variety to a long continuous run and teaches the runner to initiate surges and move from behind the pack.

DESCRIPTION
The group of runners start in single file line. After the group has been running at a leisurely pace for approximately 3 minutes, the back runner surges to the front of the line and takes over the lead. Each back runner should initiate a surge to the lead after holding the back position for 30 seconds to a minute.

Cross-Country Funnel

PURPOSE
Promotes team running while providing a controlled work-out. Athletes also learn pacing over longer distances.

DESCRIPTION
On an 8 mile run, the pace should increase each mile by 30 seconds until the middle miles, which are run at the same tempo, then the pace drops off 30 seconds with each mile. The last mile should be at same pace as the first mile.

SPECIAL INSTRUCTIONS

1st Mile	2nd Mile	3rd Mile	4th Mile	5th Mile	6th Mile	7th Mile	8th Mile
8:00	7:30	7:00	6:30	6:30	7:00	7:30	8:00

Variation: To run the 4th and 5th miles at a quicker tempo than a 30 second pick-up.

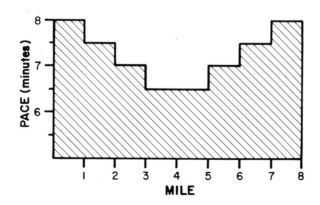

Uphill Charges
Short Hills for sprinters
Longer Hills for distance runners

PURPOSE
To increase power in the legs and strength in the quadriceps.

DESCRIPTION
With a slight forward lean, charge the hill. (Keeping the torso in the Hips Tall position and driving with the arms and legs.)

SPECIAL INSTRUCTIONS
Jog or walk back down the hill. Heart rate should be 180/minute at the top of hill. Quantity is controlled by grade and length of the hill.

■ PART B

Field Drills

■ SECTION I
Thowing Drills

DENISE WOOD

■ SUB-SECTION A *Discus*

Releasing the Discus

PURPOSE
To aid the beginner in learning the proper release of the discus.

DESCRIPTION
The athlete holds the discus comfortably in the throwing hand with the last digit of each finger placed loosely around the edge. The throwing arm and wrist are held rigid as the athlete "bowls" the discus straight ahead with minimum deviations.

SPECIAL INSTRUCTIONS
Advocating rigidity in the throwing arm often prevents the beginner from incorrectly releasing the discus from the opposite side of the hand. It also promotes flight stability.

Swinging the discus

PURPOSE

To teach relaxation of the throwing arm and to develop the concept of holding the discus while moving it but without overgripping it.

DESCRIPTION

After assuming the proper grip, the athlete swings the discus freely forward/backward and through various patterns around the body. Relaxed arm movement is encouraged to develop familiarity with the implement and confidence in the relatively loose feeling of the grip.

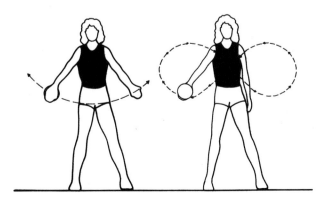

Standing Throw

PURPOSE
To learn to throw from the power position and co-ordinate essential throwing movements.

DESCRIPTION
The thrower assumes a stride position at the front of the circle with the toes pointing perpendicular to the direction of the throw and the heel of the right foot in line with the ball of the left foot. The width of the stance should allow effective body weight transfer onto the balls of the feet when moving. The thrower is guided through the basic concepts of transferring weight. Flexion/extension of the legs has subsequent effects on hip rotation and blocking. The proper co-ordination of these actions affects upper body movements and the release.

SPECIAL INSTRUCTIONS
Beginners have a tendency to limit the range of motion through which force may be applied and to neglect optimal use of the legs.

Standing Throw with Partner Resistance

PURPOSE
To promote the development of effective throwing movements through imitation of the standing throw with resistance from a partner.

DESCRIPTION
The thrower assumes a standing throw position with the body weight well back on the right foot; right arm extended. As the thrower pivots (toward the direction of the throw) and body weight transfers, the partner offers resistance by grasping the right wrist of the thrower, but allows the thrower to gradually move through the range of motion.

SPECIAL INSTRUCTIONS
If the thrower moves incorrectly, the partner should not force the thrower to find the most powerful position.

Drive to Standing Throw Position Effectively

PURPOSE
To teach the thrower to move the necessary distance from the rear of the circle to the power position with proper foot placement and balance. To develop proper timing of the feet upon landing.

DESCRIPTION
The thrower stands erect at the back of the circle with the left foot pointing in the direction of the throw. From a stride position, the left leg drives the body in the direction of the throw. The thrower executes a turn before assuming the standing throw position in the center.

SPECIAL INSTRUCTIONS
Place a mark in the circle to indicate the center. Draw the necessary markings to aid in proper placement.

This drill should be executed with and without discus.

4/4 Turn with Release

PURPOSE
To develop throwing technique by concentrating on aspects of the throw that occur once the thrower faces the throwing direction at the back of the circle.

DESCRIPTION
This drill follows the same pattern as the previous drill, except that the discus is swung backward just before the push-off of the left foot at the back of the circle and that the throw is executed.

Towel Drill

PURPOSE
To develop a more active right leg out of the back of the circle. To aid in learning proper timing of the right leg action.

DESCRIPTION
The thrower assumes the initial position as if executing a full throw. A towel is placed outside the circle and to the left of the left foot. As the athlete begins the throw, he/she focuses on the right foot kicking the towel in the direction of the throw.

SPECIAL INSTRUCTIONS
Discourage excess flexion in right knee or any vertical deviations which may adversely affect an efficient throw.

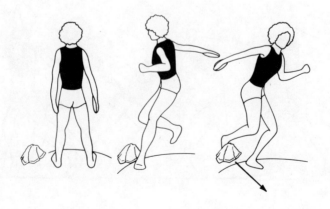

Line Drill

PURPOSE
To promote patterning the proper foot alignment and timing the touch-down of the feet. To aid in teaching balance and efficiency of movement across the circle.

DESCRIPTION
The athlete stands in a stride position with the left foot on a line on the track. In the drive to standing throw position execute a low jump turn and land in a power position. Repeat after checking timing, balance and foot alignment. After the thrower shows proficiency, execute the drill continuously down the line by continuing to turn after reaching a standing throw position. Adding a short gallop between jump turns will allow the athlete to focus on the horizon without becoming dizzy. Focus on linear aspects rather than rotational aspects of the movement.

SPECIAL INSTRUCTIONS
Timing and foot alignment are most important. Refine the length of the drive when ready.

Balance on Left

PURPOSE
To introduce balanced weight shifting to the left foot.

DESCRIPTION
The thrower assumes a stance at the back of the circle as if beginning a full throw. Weight is shifted to the left foot as the athlete executes at least a 360 turn on the ball of the left foot without losing balance.

SPECIAL INSTRUCTIONS
The drill should be used as a means of teaching the learner to attain a balanced position on the left before driving to the front foot. Beginners tend to neglect the shift over the left. This causes them to be off balance and fall to the power position, which creates problems due to the lack of control at the back of the circle. The thrower must learn to integrate the shift to the left foot with a controlled drive to the front. In the actual throw, the athlete's weight shifts to the left but is also distributed toward the direction of the throw in order to attain a lean and drive to the front.

Drive Position

PURPOSE
To allow the thrower to feel a powerful position on the left leg for the drive to the front of the circle.

DESCRIPTION
The athlete grasps a stable object for resistance as the position desired for a powerful drive to the front is assumed. Resistance allows the athlete to lean in the direction of the throw and hold the position without falling.

SPECIAL INSTRUCTIONS
The desired position of the right leg and body position may vary slightly depending upon the specific technique being learned. The drill should be adapted to specific techniques. Positions will vary slightly according to the specific demands of these techniques.

■ SUB-SECTION B   *Shotput*

Grip-Placement of the Shotput

PURPOSE
To present the beginner with a simple method of gripping and placing the shot to facilitate an effective release.

DESCRIPTION
The athlete picks up the shot from the ground using primarily the fingers and thumb, keeping it off the palm of the hand. Upon standing, the arm is raised above the head and the wrist flexed backward with the shot being supported laterally by the thumb and pinky while the remaining three fingers assume the majority of the weight of the shot. As the elbow is raised, the shot is placed against the neck and below the ear in order to keep the shot securely against the neck.

Developing the Standing Throw-Drive

PURPOSE
To establish the basic delivery position.

DESCRIPTION
The athlete assumes a straddle position facing perpendicular to the direction of the throw with the shoulders parallel to the direction of the throw and the right heel in line with the ball of the left foot. With the right arm supporting the shot against the neck and the left arm relaxed and extended in front of the trunk, the upper body turns 90° so the thrower faces in a direction opposite the throw while the hips remain perpendicular to the direction of the throw. Body weight must be well over the flexed right leg.

SPECIAL INSTRUCTIONS
Drawing a line through the middle of the circle will help the beginner develop desirable foot alignment. A stripe on the side of the shorts that remains over the center line will aid in keeping the hips in the correct position and insure production of body torque. This position should be felt with and without the shot.

Developing Weight Transfer in the Standing Throw

PURPOSE
To introduce the concepts of body weight transfer through a long range of motion and to develop effective use of the legs.

DESCRIPTION
The athlete assumes an erect straddle position with the shot against the neck in throwing position. Body weight is then transferred over the right foot through flexion of the right leg while the left leg is relaxed and extended; the shoulders remain relatively parallel to the ground. The athlete then executes the throw from this position by driving the weight with the right and allowing the left leg to extend to perform its blocking function as the weight transfers onto it.

The thrower is facing the direction of the throw upon release. Hip rotation and flexion are progressively increased and integrated properly with the weight transfer.

SPECIAL INSTRUCTIONS
This drill should be used only as a method of focusing on leg actions and weight transfer. It should be performed on a limited basis and integrated into the entire technique as soon as possible, particularly when a beginner uses too much trunk flexion and neglects the legs.

Developing the Glide

PURPOSE
To establish the basic components of the glide across the ring to the standing throw position.

DESCRIPTION
The athlete stands erect at the back of the ring facing the opposite direction of the throw. Body weight is on the right foot and the left leg is slightly flexed at the knee with the left foot touching the ground. The athlete is asked to hop backward and land on both feet simultaneously. Refine the hop by keeping it close to the surface and lengthening it while advocating simultaneous foot landing. In order to gain distance, the beginner must be guided into more leg flexion and extension with additional force and proper timing. Preliminary movement to a low position before the glide and turning the right foot and hips toward the direction of the throw upon landing can be introduced when the athlete seems ready. Eventually, the glide should take the athlete to the standing throw/delivery position.

SPECIAL INSTRUCTIONS
When landing, be sure that the body weight is well over the right foot to insure effective use of the legs. Simultaneous foot landing in the initial stages of learning is advocated for developing an effective delivery position. In actuality, the left foot contacts the ground shortly after the right. If a beginner is instructed to land on the right first then on the left, there is sometimes a misconception of how much later the left foot should land. If contact is too late, use of the right leg, hip action, and effective use of the left leg may be minimized and a variety of related problems may result.

Fence Drill

PURPOSE
To aid in learning the lower body transition from the glide to the delivery position while keeping the upper body relatively unchanged.

DESCRIPTION
The athlete grasps the fence with both hands at about hip level while standing close enough to the fence to allow as much glide distance as possible. The thrower then executes a short glide in an attempt to simulate the desired delivery position and timing while the shoulders remain parallel to the fence. The athlete should feel the separation of hips and shoulders and potential power of the right leg.

SPECIAL INSTRUCTIONS
By pivoting on the ball of the right foot toward the direction of the throw, the hips will turn toward the direction of the throw and the athlete may develop more flexibility for additional torque production.

Glide With Partner Resistance

PURPOSE
To help the athlete avoid premature shoulder turn in the direction of throw and to keep the body weight well over the right foot.

DESCRIPTION
The performer assumes a stance at the back of the circle in preparation for a glide while a partner grasps the performer's left wrist. As the performer executes the glide, the partner moves with the thrower but offers resistance if the shoulders begin to turn prematurely. Upon landing in the delivery position, the partner checks the weight distribution of the performer and, if the weight is undesirably off the right foot, forces the performer to shift back over the right. The drill may be repeated with and without the shot.

SPECIAL INSTRUCTIONS
The drill should not be repeated excessively and integration of these positions into the entire throw is advised. Alternating the drill with full throws is often helpful until the movement is executed automatically in the full throw.

Glide to Medicine Ball

PURPOSE
To help the athlete efficiently extend the left leg toward the board in the desired direction.

DESCRIPTION
The athlete executes a glide from the rear of the ring while attempting to push the medicine ball which is placed at the center of the front of the ring. If the ball is pushed directly forward, the athlete has executed a glide with a low, efficient left leg extension. This drill will help in preventing vertical deviations or "bucket" problems.

SPECIAL INSTRUCTIONS
This drill may be done with and without the shot. The movement should be integrated into the whole throw as soon as possible.

Learning the Reverse

PURPOSE
To teach the beginner to avoid fouling after releasing the shot.

DESCRIPTION
The athlete executes a standing throw without a reverse, emphasizing maximum effort with a powerful breaking action from the left leg. On the next throw, the athlete is asked to feel that same power and block, but to use so much effort that a foul would occur without reverse. The athlete continues to throw, attempting to reverse at the precise moment maximum effort has been applied and before it is too late to save the throw. The right foot should replace the left at the board, and the left leg is thrown back to counter balance the upper body.

SPECIAL INSTRUCTIONS
Some athletes may need to practice the reverse without a shot to simplify the task. This way the reverse alone may be focused on, rather than first focusing on the throw and then the reverse.

Goal Post Drill

PURPOSE
To aid in teaching the athlete how to use the whole body to attain optimal lift in the throw.

DESCRIPTION
The athlete may execute standing throws or glides, propelling the shot over a cross bar or a goal post. Varying the distance to the goal post will cause the athlete to adapt to releasing the shot at different angles.

Use of whole body in projecting the shot at an optimal angle should be advocated.

SPECIAL INSTRUCTIONS
Athletes should be given as much feedback as possible to facilitate attainment of the desired results.

■ SUB-SECTION C *Javelin*

Gripping the Javelin

PURPOSE
To teach the beginner a practical grip for throwing the javelin.

DESCRIPTION
The athlete holds the javelin on the front portion of the shaft with the left hand. The right hand grips the back portion of the shaft with the palm up. The athlete slides the javelin down the palm until the middle finger reaches the binding. The javelin is then supported by the thumb and last two digits of the middle finger, which are behind the binding. While the index finger supports the shaft from below, the remaining fingers wrap over the binding to stabilize the javelin in the palm of the hand.

SPECIAL INSTRUCTIONS
If the "V" or "fork" grip is desired, the index finger supports the javelin on the thumb side. The grip described in this drill offers the advantage of the longer lever of the middle finger, which has a positive affect upon the rotation of the javelin around the long axis (this enhances flight stability). In addition, the index finger acts as a control during the carry.

These two are the grips most frequently employed by outstanding throwers today.

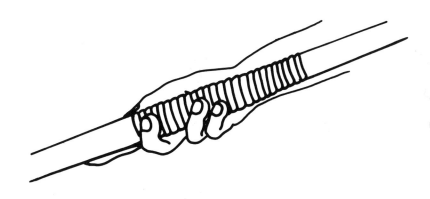

"C" Position Drill

PURPOSE
To simulate the delivery position and to aid in trunk flexibility.

DESCRIPTION
The thrower places the tip of the javelin against some solid object (fence, tree) that will stabilize it at release height. The right leg is extended forward as the left leg assumes its blocking position. The back is well arched in a "C" position. The shoulders and hips are both facing in the direction of the throw.

Javelin Standing Throw from Static Position

PURPOSE

To teach the basic sequence of movements immediately before the release and to provide a simple orientation to the throw.

DESCRIPTION

Standing in a forward stride position, the upper body is turned to the right until the shoulders point in the throwing direction. The right arm is comfortably extended and the javelin is parallel to the ground at head level. Body weight is shifted onto the right leg which is slightly flexed. A throw is executed through the extension of the right leg which initiates a hip rotation in the direction of the throw. The arm should come through as a result of leg and hip actions. The left leg extends and brakes the momentum of the lower body. The right leg should be fully extended before it leaves the ground to follow through.

SPECIAL INSTRUCTIONS

The drill should not be used excessively. Once the basic concepts are introduced and the athlete performs acceptably, advanced drills should be undertaken.

Walking Step into Throwing Position

PURPOSE
To teach the beginner the proper throwing motion when momentum is introduced.

DESCRIPTION
The athlete assumes a stride position with the right foot slightly to the right and in front of the left; the throwing arm is extended. The athlete takes one step into the throwing position and executes the throw.

SPECIAL INSTRUCTIONS
The body should have some backward lean going into the throwing position so the beginner can feel effective use of the right leg and prepare for backward inclination of the trunk. This action allows longer application of force from the right leg as the hips move quickly over the right foot.

Impulse Stride to Throwing Position/Throw

PURPOSE
To introduce and incorporate the impulse stride into the throw.

DESCRIPTION
The athlete assumes a similar position to the static standing throw with the weight well over the right foot. The weight is then taken onto the left leg at which time the thrower bounds (executing the "crossover") into the standing throw position. Upon landing, the weight should be well over the right foot and the left foot should have come through and planted as quickly as possible. After checking this position, the drill is repeated with the addition or the execution of the throw.

SPECIAL INSTRUCTIONS
It is not unusual for learners to plant the left foot too late for it to function optimally. The impulse stride should be forceful enough to allow time for the left foot to pass the right in the air and to touch down soon after the right foot. It should be low and long. The right knee should be well flexed when taking the body weight since a high position would delay the left foot plant.

5 Stride Drill

PURPOSE
To teach the beginner the transition from the approach to the throw (last 5 steps).

DESCRIPTION
The thrower stands erect with both feet together and the javelin held in the carry position. The first step is taken onto the left foot, which points in the direction of the throw. The second step is taken onto the right foot which turns slightly to the right as the javelin withdrawal is initiated. By this time the left foot is grounded (step 3) and begins to execute the impulse stride into the throwing position (steps 4&5). The javelin is fully withdrawn upon landing on the right foot which is turned to the right of the throwing direction. The body is inclined well back and the hips are turned to the right to allow optimal use of the lower body through a long range of motion. The throw is executed as previously described.

SPECIAL INSTRUCTIONS
The impulse stride initiated from the left foot on step 3 should be elongated. As the athlete becomes comfortable walking through the steps, gradually add speed and eventually a jog to the last 5 steps. It is sometimes helpful to have the athlete count the last 5 steps aloud as they are performed in order to define them at the end of the approach.

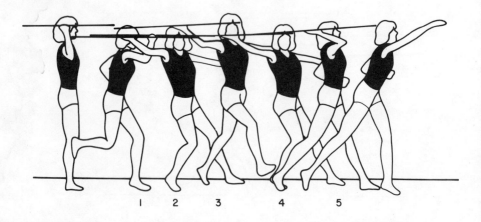

                I   2   3   4   5

Withdrawal Drill

PURPOSE
To pattern the withdrawal or the javelin so that the correct movements become properly timed and automatic.

DESCRIPTION
The athlete jogs holding the javelin in the carry position. The athlete begins the withdrawal as weight is taken onto the left foot and completes the withdrawal when the next stride is completed. The drill is repeated until timing of the withdrawal is automatic.

SPECIAL INSTRUCTIONS
The drill should be executed more quickly as the athlete progresses. It should also be integrated with the crossover (impulse stride) and throw as soon as possible.

Javelin Bounds

PURPOSE
To allow the thrower to practice the "crossover" repeatedly with the javelin fully withdrawn.

DESCRIPTION
The thrower assumes a position with the weight well over the right foot, the body turned to the right and the arms extended. The "crossover" step is repeated with an even rhythm for about 20-30 yards. The javelin is kept in the same position as if the actual "crossover" during a 5-stride approach was being executed. The bounds should be long and the knees should be high as the bounds are executed. As the right knee comes forward, the left arm moves in front of the body.

SPECIAL INSTRUCTIONS
Since this drill is executed with an even rhythm, it does not simulate the actual throwing rhythm. This drill allows the thrower to concentrate on executing an effective impulse stride with optimal length. Integration of the impulse stride with a quick plant of the left foot is essential. The ability to execute long and powerful bounds will allow sufficient time for the left leg to pass the right in the air and the left foot to plant quickly.

Double Leg Bounds over Barriers

PURPOSE
To teach the athlete to explode and react to various angles of landing and trajectory.

DESCRIPTION
The throwers execute double leg bounds (jumps) over bariers of varying heights/distances.

SPECIAL INSTRUCTIONS
Double leg bounds help the athlete learn to project her body at various angles and react quickly in adapting to a new angle of projection. This can assist the thrower to change the trajectory angle of the implement through use of the whole body rather than through use of the arm.

Throwing Weighted Objects

PURPOSE
To allow the athlete to execute various drills/throws without the javelin to enhance concentration on movements rather than distance.

DESCRIPTION
The thrower executes standing throws, impulse strides with throw and other drills using small weighted balls or other objects. This allows the athlete to focus on various aspects of the throw without concern for the height or distance. This is particularly helpful in teaching the overhand throw to the beginner.

Triple Jumps/Variations

PURPOSE
To increase explosiveness and co-ordination for throwers.

DESCRIPTION
From a standing position the athlete executes triple jumps and variations (on grass or mats). They may be done in any combinations: HOP, STEP, JUMP—HOP, HOP, STEP, JUMP—HOP, STEP, STEP, JUMP—HOP, HOP, STEP, STEP, JUMP—HOP, HOP, STEP, STEP, JUMP—HOP, HOP, STEP, STEP, JUMP, JUMP.

SPECIAL INSTRUCTIONS
This drill may be done competitively. Using the arms and exaggerating every phase of the series should be advocated.

■ SUB-SECTION D *Medicine Ball*

Medicine Ball Exercises

PURPOSE
To develop explosiveness, strength, flexibility and coordination through executing various exercises with a medicine ball.

DESCRIPTION
The following diagrams show medicine ball exercises that are effective in offering resistance through various ranges of motion. Many of these exercises are particularly helpful in developing the muscles of the trunk and abdominal area. Those exercises in which the ball is released should be performed explosively.

■ SECTION II

Jumping Drills

LOREN SEAGRAVE

INTRODUCTION TO PLYOMETRICS

Plyometrics is a word that was synthesized to describe a battery of drills and exercises known under the subcategory names of skipping, bounding, hopping and depth jumping. The design of these tasks is constructed to positively affect certain physiological parameters that govern physical performance capability. The quality of a complex explosive motor activity is determined by two main factors. The physiological preparedness of the effector organ, which in this case is the muscle, and the degree of neuromuscular coordination and ability of the central nervous system to recruit the large fast twitch motor units.

Plyometrics can positively effect change in both parameters. The physiological preparedness of the muscle can be simply broken down to how much force is generated during maximal contraction of the muscle.

Weight training is used to develop and enhance the basal strength level muscle. Plyometrics are used in conjunction with weight training and other progressive resistance exercises. The additional benefit of plyometric training lies in the application of the resistance force. Characteristically, plyometrics use force generated by gravity acting upon the weight of the body or the body plus additional weight.

As in depth jumping, the athlete jumps down from a prescribed height. Upon ground impact, the task is to respond immediately by trying to jump up from the ground. As the athlete lands, the muscles are stretched very quickly,albeit a very small amount. This stretch elicits the myotonic reflex (stretch reflex). The quick stretch of the muscle spindle sends a stimulus through the sensory nervous system to the spinal cord. The sensory neuron synapses directly onto a motor neuron which innervates motor units in the antagonistic muscle. This reflex firing of the antagonistic muscle groups is added to the conscious innervation, producing a greater total stimulus to the muscle. This yields a greater response in strength development, through increasing the physiological preparedness of the muscle.

Perhaps of greater importance is the value of plyometrics in "teaching" the neuro-muscular system how to apply a great amount of force over a shortened period of time. When force is measured over time the result is power.

The force application or impulse must be applied over the shortest time frame physiologically possible to maximize performance. Using a system of gradually reducing the ground contact time by increasing the athletes velocity, the demands on the central nervous system require a better integration of stimuli to the muscle. In addition, the demands on the neuromuscular system are very specific to running and jumping. This promotes an increased neuro-muscular coordination and responsiveness.

Lastly, the concept of using jump facilitated training to change the force production curve, has opened interesting possibilities. This topic will not be discussed within the course of this text.

Plyometrics should be performed on a resilient, yet not totally shock absorbant material. This is especially true during the top competitive season, when the response characteristics of the surface have a great deal to do with the resultant ground contact time and force transmission. Early season training should be done on an even grass or artificial grass surface. This should gradually progress to a resilient artificial track surface.

Exploding Harvards

PURPOSE
This exercise is one of the first progressions used to introduce the athlete to plyometric training. The reduced impact of landing allows the athlete to ease into this new type of training.

DESCRIPTION
Boxes or a step of sufficient height to put the athlete's knee angle between 80° and 120° is most desirable. A knee angle of much less than 90° puts undue stress on the knee joint and the patellar tendon.

The athlete places one foot on the box. The body is forward so as to put as much weight over the flexed leg as possible. The arms are carried in a sprint position. The exercise is begun by a powerful extension of the hip joint and a simultaneous thrust from the arms. The hips are projected directly upward over the leg applying the force. The object is to attain maximum height. While the body is in an airborn "Hips Tall" position, the passive leg takes the place of the active leg in catching the body and returning it to the starting position. As soon as the now passive leg touches the ground, the active leg can explode. The goal of this phase of the exercise is to minimize the ground contact time of the non-working leg. The arms are driven synchronously with the legs.

Active Sprint Skipping

PURPOSE
This plyometric activity has a high degree of specificity with regard to sprinting. Ground contact time can be made very short yet still demand a very powerful impulse.

DESCRIPTION
This drill is nothing more than trying to skip, reaching the greatest velocity possible. Emphasis is placed on a vigorous, full range of motion with the arms. Also, a very active, pulling back action is essential in the optimal development of the hamstrings and gluts.

SPECIAL INSTRUCTIONS
To add extra impetus to training, time various distances 30 meters, 50 meters and 100 meters from a fly. To add a more head to head competitive nature to the training, race from a standing start position over various distances from 30 meters to 100 meters.

High Skip Every Third

PURPOSE
This drill allows the athlete to add increased velocity to the plyometric drill, demanding that the impulse must be of shorter duration to achieve the desired result. This exercise is also useful for working on the take-off impulse in the long jump and to some extent the high jump. When used with long jumpers extreme care must be taken to insure a very active plant. The forward and upward projection of the hips is essential to prevent the braking effect inherent in doing pop-ups purely for height.

DESCRIPTION
The athlete performs active skipping. Every third stride is an explosive pop-up. The arms are driven vigorously and synchronously with the high skip. Emphasis is placed on an active plant, resulting in a forward and upward projection of the hips. The impulse is derived from power hip extension. The coach should give feedback to minimize reaching out into the plant.

Swedish Hops

PURPOSE

This exercise emphasizes the vertical component of the transfer rather than the velocity sparing horizontal component. It may be used for all explosive athletes but is particularly well suited to high jumpers, triple jumpers, throwers and long jumpers.

DESCRIPTION

This action resembles a continuous high skipping. The drive upward of the swing leg and deliberate arm action are preceeded by an active plant. Care is taken not to reach out in front of the body, rather to explode into the ground yielding the desired height.

Low Slow Bounding

PURPOSE

The application of force through a greater range of joint motion than is encountered in sprinting is desirable. The importance of stressing the muscular system through a full range of motion not only strengthens the muscles and creates greater responsiveness at all joint angles, but also enhances dynamic flexibility.

DESCRIPTION

Starting in a ¾ crouch or ¾ squat position, body balance is lost by slightly falling forward. At a moment before total control is lost the arms drive in an exaggerated sprint form moving through a greater than normal range. Simultaneously, a forceful drive from the hip extensors projects the hips forward. In response, the other leg flexes, driving the knee forward and upward and coming to an abrupt halt at a position parallel to the ground. A brief float phase ensues followed by a powerful extension of the swing leg resulting in low forward projection of the hips.

Power Bounding

PURPOSE
The greater specificity to running is used to maximize the power potential of the athlete. Although ground contact time is significantly greater than in sprinting, the advantage of force application through the entire range of hip extension is very desirable. All the propulsive force should be realized from behind the athlete and ideally little reaching out in front of the athlete resulting in braking forces.

DESCRIPTION
A small jog-in adds momentum and velocity to the system. The body is in a "hips tall" position. The torso and trunk are also tall. The action described in the low slow bounding is identical. The foot strike is more on a flat foot. The foot strike is very active in that the direction of the foot is backward at ground contact. The floating feeling of the flight phase is long, so that the athlete feels that the ground is coming up to meet the explosive response of the extending leg.

Speed Bounding

PURPOSE

The further increase in velocity necessitates a quicker application of force to the ground. The shorter ground contact time and full range of force application from extension of the hip transfers to a greater stride length during sprinting.

In addition, the transmission of forces through the musculoskeletal system is made more efficient by "teaching" the gastrosoleal complex to fire before ground contact. This minimizes the force lost to absorption. The foot is not allowed to dorsiflex on ground contact resulting in the heel not appreciably touching the ground.

DESCRIPTION

This plyometric is the hybrid of power bounding and power sprinting. The stride frequency is increased so that the float phase is diminished, yet is still noticeably present. The plant of the foot is very active resulting in conserved horizontal velocity. No reaching out in front by the lower leg should be noticeable. Contact is further forward toward the ball of the foot rather than flat as in power bounding. A slightly greater run in is used to increase the velocity of the exercise.

Hurdle Hops

PURPOSE

The addition of barriers obviates a greater vertical component in the hop, which requires a more abrupt breaking impulse. The quadriceps are particularly involved in this exercise, which is especially beneficial to high jumpers, throwers and horizontal jumpers. The combination of alternating a Hurdle Hop with a Double Leg Hop integrates tasks, one being of a greater vertical nature, the other emphasizing conserving the horizontal component.

DESCRIPTION

Hurdles or other suitable soft barriers are placed 2.00 meters to 2.50 meters apart. A suitable height is selected commensurate with the athlete's level of conditioning and ability. This may vary from 24" to 36". Using a double hop action, the athlete hops over the barrier. Initially there may be a pause between barriers. This will lead to intermediate preparatory hops before clearing each barrier. Finally the plyometric activity of response upon impact will be reached.

Run-Run-Bound

PURPOSE

The additional impetus of even greater velocity demands a shorter impulse, which must be executed through a full range of motion.

DESCRIPTION

The athlete takes an easy three to five step run into a bound stride. The next two successive strides are very quick strides, yet are not full running strides. The next step is a full bounding stride. The run-run-bound rhythm allows the athlete to alternate legs with each bounding stride.

SPECIAL INSTRUCTIONS

Although it may seem appropriate to use a hurdle rhythm in this drill, it should be avoided. The take-off for bounding is significantly different from the hurdle take off so that a negative transfer of motor patterns could result.

Drum Major

PURPOSE
The plyometric nature of this activity gives an additional benefit to this dynamic flexibility exercise. The stress placed on the body's internal hip flexors and abdominal musculature in a dynamic setting is also useful to the sprinter.

DESCRIPTION
Every major marching band has a flamboyant drum major who preceeds the band. At one point in the routine, they stop and on a spot kick their legs high in the air in a goose step action. This is the basis of the drill. The athlete attempts to keep a forward posture of the torso. A very forceful thigh extension pops the ball of the foot onto the ground. One goal of this drill is to maximize ground response and minimize ground contact time.

SPECIAL INSTRUCTIONS
This drill is best used in a circuit of ground reaction drills and sprint mechanics drills.

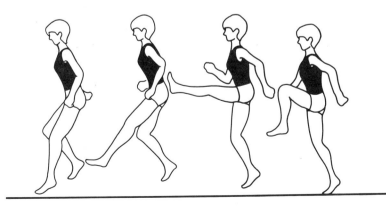

Straight Leg Bounds

PURPOSE

This drill brings into play the hip extension action of the hamstring group. The added contribution of the gluteus and calves makes it an excellent pulling action to strengthen muscle weaknesses.

DESCRIPTION

A small jog begins the drill. The athlete, with the leg extended at the knee joint, forcefully extends this straightened leg from the hip joint. The resultant action causes the foot to strike the ground with high backward speed. The ground contact is slightly in front of the body, yet the support through the entire stride is only on the ball of the foot. The tempo should be very quick. The torso should be forward and the arm swing should emulate the sprint action. The athlete should feel as though they are pulling the ground past them.

Single Leg Hop

PURPOSE

This exercise is the next step of loading in a progressive plyometric system. The added complexity stresses the neural recruitment of motor units as well as promoting coordinated sprint and power movements.

DESCRIPTION

The athlete places one leg before the other. The front leg is the hopping leg. With a powerful thrust, the athlete drives the hips up and forward. The hopping leg is recovered as in sprinting, so the heel is pulled to the buttocks followed by the knee swinging forward and up in a cyclical action. When the thigh is parallel, the leg is abruptly extended from the thigh and actively pulled backward to strike the ground with high backward foot speed. The landing is on the flat of the foot. The opposite leg cycles as if it were being used, yet doesn't contact the ground. This helps balance the action. The arms drive in an asynchronous rhythm to maximize force application and facilitate recovery time of the hopping leg.

SPECIAL INSTRUCTIONS

To learn this action and provide a less stressful intermediate in the progression, a Crazy Hop drill can be employed, which is a single leg hop done on one spot. Until the athlete is able to master the action and integrate a horizontal component only vertical forces are undertaken. This eliminates the severe shearing forces to the leg. It also minimizes the risk of injury to young inexperienced athletes. Hop Test: The evaluation of the athletes proficiency in executing a 30 meter single leg hop test where the time and number of steps are recorded is a very good parameter for measuring progress in achieving sprint power as well as neuro-muscular coordination and integration.

Continuous Triple Jump

PURPOSE
This movement series develops neuro-muscular power and coordination in both legs as well as the specific action of moving from one leg to the other.

DESCRIPTION
The cyclical leg action described in the single leg hop is used in each phase of the continuous triple jump. The difference involves alternating legs in a prescribed pattern. The cadance and pattern used goes R-R-L-L-R-R-L-L. The plyometric actions that are incorporated into the continuous triple jump corresponding to the preceeding cadence are Hop-Bound-Hop-BoundHop-Bound-Hop. A useful variation of this pattern is Hop-Hop-Bound-Hop-Hop-Bound.

Double Leg Hops

PURPOSE
This exercise employs various explosive responses from back, gluteal and quadriceps muscles and promotes neuro factors. The statistics which should be recorded are, distance for ten maximal hops, time and number of hops to cover a twenty to thirty meter distance. Another parameter to record is the distance achieved in ten hops on the way to twenty or thirty meters timed. This can then be compared with the ten maximal hop distance to evaluate the coordination and integration processes.

DESCRIPTION
This action involves a series of successive standing broad jumps. If the task orientation is "See how far you can go with ten hops," the function is a pure strength/power design. A pause is taken after each landing, the athlete regroups and another powerful jump is performed. When a time element is added such that the task becomes "how fast and in how few steps can you cover a 20 meter distance," a plyometric component comes into play. As a result, the landing action becomes much more active and the ground contact time is reduced. This leads to a more complete stimulus of the central and peripheral nervous system.

Plyometrics for Jumpers (Depth Jumping)

PURPOSE
To achieve a more powerful muscle contraction.

DESCRIPTION
Single leg and double leg box jumping should be included in workouts after a basic groundwork of conditioning is established (3-4 weeks).

Single jumps can start off a box roughly 12" high. The athlete should start on the box, jump down to the grass, and immediately spring back up to another box. Jumps should be taken off the dominant and non-dominant legs. A workout could start with 5 repetitions off each leg and increase as the athlete's strength and coordination develops. Double legged jumps can be made off boxes 18"-24" high, depending on the athlete's strength. A workout could start with 10 repetitions and increase with experience and strength development.

The coach must emphasize quickness off the ground to best utilize these drills. A quick double arm punch and fast aggressive knee drive also make the drill more effective.

SPECIAL INSTRUCTIONS
Low box-ground-low box, low box-ground-high box, low box-groundhigh box-ground-low box, high box-ground-high box-ground-low box, etc.

Depth jumping only needs to be done 1-2 times a week with 1 or 2 days between sessions for muscle recovery. Since this training overloads the muscles, athletes will need 10 to 14 days recovery from this type of training before very important meets.

Sue Humphreys

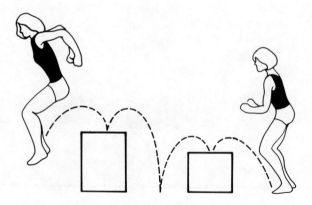

■ SUB-SECTION B
Sue Humphrey

Long Jump and High Jump

Beginner-Flop Technique

PURPOSE
To teach the flop form to a beginner.

DESCRIPTIONS
Decide on the take-off foot (take a running jump and see what foot is used to take off).

Mark a curved approach on each side of the apron with tape (this should be a guide only).

Execute a scissors jump using a 5-step curved approach to a sitting landing position on the pit, then a back landing position.

Do a scissors jump as above concentrating on a free knee drive up.

The double arm action is started going into the last step. For a right footed jumper, the left foot is forward on the second to last step and the right arm is forward. Keep the right arm forward as the jumper goes into the final step, which is right foot and left arm forward. Now both arms are in front of the body, "pinch" the elbows back and punch the arms together forward and upward to shoulder height as the free knee (Left) is being driven up to parallel as quickly as possible.

Various Flop Technique Drills

PURPOSE
To teach the back layout (flop) high jump technique.

DESCRIPTIONS
Back rolls on high gym mats or a trampoline from a standing start.

Back pull-overs with a partner for flexibility. Mirror practice the double arm blocking action and lead knee vertical drive. This should be also walked and jogged through.

Place the bar at the jumper's waist height, have her stand with her back to the bar, slightly flex her knees, jump up and then layout over the bar. This drill will encourage vertical lift to clear the bar. A double arm punch will help as the jumper jumps up.

Circle runs in the direction of the jumper's curve so she can feel what a true curve feels like, circle 8 runs in the direction of the jumper's curve.

Various Types of High Jumping Practices

PURPOSE

To work on the many phases of the jump and approach.

DESCRIPTION

Full approaches (9-10 steps for example). The purpose is to achieve the feeling or "tempo" of an approach and speed the jumper can control when jumping. The athlete should take a jump of average height at the end of the approach. Short approaches (3-5 steps). The purpose is to work on a specific technique area. This type of drill should not be used excessively. Full approaches with a jump should be used most of the time. The bar should be set at an average height for short approaches too.

Technique jumping. The purpose is to take 10-15 jumps at average and above average heights to develop various aspects of the approach, take-off, and bar action movements.

Height jumping. The purpose is to jump at higher heights for experience so when the jumper faces these heights in a meet the bar won't appear so high. Take a few jumps for warmup at a clearable height, move the bar up to a height not usually cleared in meets, jump at it 4-6 times even if all attempts are missed. Then evaluate each jump for its positive and negative points.

Hitch-Kick Long Jump

PURPOSE
To learn the different steps in the hitch-kick style of jumping.

DESCRIPTION
The following drills are for a left footed jumper-a right footed jumper can just change the feet labels to the opposite foot.

Step 1.
Drive the right knee up and forward until it's parallel to the ground.
Drive the left arm forward flexed until the hand is at eye level.

The right arm stays flexed at the hip level. The left leg just follows the body into the pit. Land on the right foot with the knee flexed to absorb the weight.

Step 2.

Follow step 1 and then the right leg extends downward and slightly passes the body midline (like a bike pedaling action).

The right arm is driven back and then up over the head. The left leg is brought forward with the knee flexed and continues forward until the thigh is parallel with the ground.

The upper body stays upright and tall during steps 1 & 2.

The left arm is driven back and upwards.

Land with the left leg forward and the right leg back.

Step 3.

Follow steps 1 & 2 then the right leg comes forward with the knee flexed, the heel close to the buttocks, and extends forward.

The right arm comes forward, then is thrust backwards, and quickly brought forward at the landing.

The left leg extends into the pit.

The left arm joins the right in its forward, backward, and forward action.

Land with the legs extended in a sitting position.

Endurance jumping

PURPOSE
To develop endurance and consistancy at heights and to get ready for long drawn-out competitions.

DESCRIPTION
Start with the bar 6" below the jumper's seasonal best, jump and take three attempts if needed to clear the height, then move the bar up 2" at a time. When a height that can't be cleared in three attempts is reached, move the bar down 1" and take some jumps. When a clearable height is reached go back up 2"—judgement by the coach is needed on the various heights and length of practice. The session should end with a height the jumper has cleared. Usually 20-25 jumps are taken during this type of practice over a 1½-2 hour period. Breaks should be taken to simulate meet conditions.

The following is an example for a 6' jumper:

5'6	5'8	5'10	6'0	5'11	5'10	5'9	5'11	6'0	6'1	5'11
OX	X	OOX	OOO	OX	X	X	OX	OX	OOO	OOX

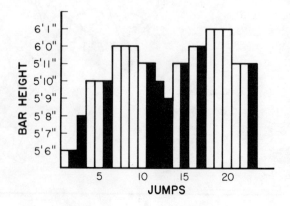

Forward Height in Long Jump

PURPOSE
To develop a tall body position during the jump.

DESCRIPTION
Put two pole vault standards on either side of the pit about 10′ from the board. A string or light rope with a towel or object hanging down should be hung between the two standards. The jumper takes a short approach, takes-off from the board or a closer predetermined mark, and tries to reach her head and shoulders toward the hanging object.

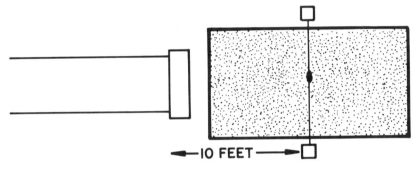

Long Jump Pop-Ups

PURPOSE
To practice the hitch-kick or hand action in the air from a short run-up.

DESCRIPTION
The jumper uses a short approach, either 5-7 strides. She runs toward the pit using good, controlled speed. The coach and athlete should decide if the jumper is to take-off from the board or a mark closer to the pit. The jumper takes off just as she would in a regular jump and completes her "in the air" action. The coach should watch and have the jumper work on the various parts of the long jump technique. If the jumper is learning a new form, a low box might be used at take-off. The jumper runs up as before and steps up on the box for take-off and completes her action with this added height. Once the action is learned, take the box away so the extra height doesn't become a crutch.

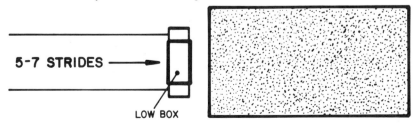

Weight Lifting for Jumpers

PURPOSE
To develop, improve, and increase the strength and power needed for jumping.

DESCRIPTION
Phase I lasts 4 weeks. Complete 12 repetitions at each circuit station, start at 40-60% of the current max, increase weight weekly, lift 3 times a week. Circuit: Leg press, shoulder press, leg curls, bent knee situps, bench press, good mornings or back extentions, arm curls, pulldowns.

Phase II lasts 4-8 weeks. Using 60% of the current maximum ability, add weight weekly, lifting 3 times a week.

Major lifts: cleans 3 sets × 6 reps, shoulder press 3×10, ¼-½ squats, 3×10, pulldowns 3×10, dead lift 3×10, sit-ups 3×20, arm curls 3×10, single legged leg curls 3×10. Add supplemental exercises, if you wish.

Phase III lasts 6-8 weeks. Using 75-80% of the current maximum capacity, add weight weekly, lifting 2-3 times a week. Major lifts: cleans 4 sets × 5 reps, bench press 4×5, back and front squats 4×5 (alternate lifts), pulldowns 4×5, situps 3×20, arm curls 4×5, single legged leg curls 4×5. Add supplementals as needed.

Phase IV lasts 2-3 weeks and is the peaking phase. Pyramid or use 75%-85% of the current maximum capacity, add weight weekly, lifting 1-2 times a week. Lifts: cleans 2 sets × 6 reps or pyramid, pull downs, front and back squats, bench press, single legged leg curls.

When planning these phases start with phase IV and work backwards to fit in the other phases.

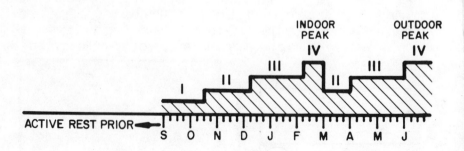